Become an Alpha Male

How to Become an Alpha Male to Gain Respect, Attract Women and Show that you're the Boss

Leo Turati

SOUTHSHORE
PUBLICATIONS & DISTRIBUTION

www.southshorepublications.com

ISBN- 978-1512397963

ISBN-10: 1512397962

Leo Turati

CONTENTS

1. INTRODUCTION

So you want to be an alpha male? Well, you have just found the perfect book for you.

The things that come to mind when I think of an alpha male is someone who is a leader and someone who is powerful. Overall, someone who demands respect from the people around him.

As humans, we may have come a long way from our rather hairy ancestors but, we still have various animalistic instincts hardwired into our brains. These instincts dictate much of our behavior on a subconscious level. They also dictate how we judge others, and how we are judged in return.

In the animal kingdom the alpha male gets the best of everything. He gets his pick of the females, his pick of the food, his pick of the territory and pretty much anything else for that matter. It simply doesn't get better than being the alpha male.

Humans are exactly the same and women are attracted to modern versions of alpha males. Take celebrities, people with high levels of power and successful people, even men with muscular builds are more attractive to women because they look more powerful and more like an alpha male. In our society, men with money are also powerful and therefore they are more of an alpha male. As you will find out being an alpha male actually increases you chance of being successful in the first place too.

By understanding and harnessing our inner animalistic instincts we can give off an air of dominance that will send out powerful signals. This will lead everyone around you to respect you as an alpha male.

So get ready to learn the hidden laws of dominance and learn rule the jungle!

2. THE ALPHA MALE CODE

The first thing I want to do before I get into the subtle tricks, body language and actions we can use to subconsciously plant the idea into people's heads that we are the alpha male, I want to get the basics covered.

For me, being a modern alpha male isn't just about being a tough guy. It's more about demanding respect in other ways. If you want respect, the first requirement is that you need to be a decent guy in general. No one is going to respect a douche bag.

So I have come up with this modern day alpha male code of conduct so that you can make sure you're hitting all of these points before moving onto the subconscious stuff.

You need to have self-respect and dignity. After all, who is going to respect you if you don't respect yourself? The easiest way to do this is to just take a bit more pride in yourself and the elevated self-respect will follow. Being proud isn't always a bad thing. You need a good balance.

If you're a doormat and you let people walk all over you then you will have no self-respect. If you're too proud to ever admit you're wrong, no one else will respect you. The trick is finding that line right down the middle.

Being proud and having self-respect has an effect on every aspect of our lives, from the way we interact with other people to what we post on our social networks. When I scroll through my newsfeed I see people posting needy statuses and photos where the person is obviously crying out for attention and gratification. These are not something that someone who has pride in themselves would post out to the world. Remember, everything you post online is a reflection of yourself and will alter people's opinions of you.

Be compassionate towards others. Alpha males classically help out other members of the group and look after their subordinates. It's really important that you help others and that you're a kind person if you want to be seen as a true alpha male. There's a lot of bad people in the world and these people are never respected for the right reasons, when they are respected it's usually out of fear. Fear will buy a horrible person respect in the short term, but it won't be genuine and it won't last. So be a compassionate person that people will say good things about.

Loyalty is one of the most important traits anybody can possess. If you want people to respect you, you will need to be a loyal person. If people see you saying a lot of negative things about your friends behind their back and then being nice to their face for example, that will show you are an un-loyal person and they will actually lose respect for you for doing that and also see you as being less trustworthy.

Keep your word. This is a classic and is referenced constantly in films and TV shows. If you are a man of your word you are generally more respected and people know you are someone who can be relied on. I practice this one heavily. If I say I am going to be somewhere or do something, even if it comes to it and I really can't be bothered, I still do it because I said I would. It's a very simple concept and one that a lot of people seem to fail at these days for some reason. So if you're someone that cancels plans a lot and you let people down, you really need to work on this one.

You need to be motivated and confident in your path in life. If you just float through life in a dead end job never really doing anything noteworthy, people will lose respect for you as a man. Real men have their priorities straight and are motivated to get/keep their life moving along the way they want it to. This is very important when it comes to women as they love a man who is grounded and has motivation to better himself. This is a great way of getting people to respect you.

Remember, to be motivated and have a clear path in life, you don't need to be in the best place right now. As long as people can see that you're moving in the right direction and that you're taking action to make it happen then this will make people see you as the kind of man who gets things done.

This motivation should be driven by an inner desire and a passion. Being passionate about something is infectious to people around you. When people can see you are passionate about something they are drawn to you and they may well even see you as being inspiring. This is a great way to earn respect and is also majorly important when it comes to women, because they love a guy who is passionate.

Confidence is very important in the modern day alpha male. Battling through any nerves and giving off an air of confidence will make people feel like we are a natural leader and that we can be relied on when others may shy away from things. The great thing about this, is that you don't even really need to do anything any different to how you're doing it now, just be confident about the things you're doing and it will gain you instant respect.

You should also remember that respect is a two way street. You need to show respect to others in order to get it in return. If you disrespect people publicly and humiliate them, it may well get other people to see you as a dominant figure but they will also think you're a horrible person, which will lose you respect in the long term. Also the person that you disrespected will have a very hard time respecting you in the future simply because they don't like you.

I'm not saying you need to be a pushover and agree with other people all of the time to ensure that they don't dislike you. What you can do however is to disagree in a courteous way and be respectful of their point of view even if you don't agree with it. By showing them this respect, they will respect you more in return.

So take pride in yourself, have self-respect, be compassionate and kind. Be loyal, stick to your word, be motivated, be passionate, be confident and be respectful of others. Do all of this and you will have mastered the modern alpha male code.

This is just the basis of gaining respect, but there is a lot more we can do from this point to cement our position as alpha male. We can take some great lessons from our cousins in the ape world. So let's take a look at what we can learn from them and how we can implement these lessons into our modern day lives.

Leo Turati

3. APPEARANCE AND BODY LANGUAGE

Statistics show that communication is only about 7% of what you say, 93% is communicated by your body language. So, to be an alpha male, we are definitely going to have to work on our appearance and body language.

Despite what women might tell you, when it comes to being an alpha male, size definitely matters. If you were shown a group of gorillas and told to point out the alpha male, how would you tell which one it was? Well obviously you would point straight to the biggest, meanest looking one.

Luckily for us we aren't gorillas, so we don't have to be the biggest, toughest guy to be an alpha male in today's world. In fact, some primates don't always have to be the biggest to be the alpha male of the group but they will always puff themselves up and stand as tall as they can to make themselves look as big as possible.

Interesting fact for you, Chimps actually raise their hair in order to puff themselves out and make themselves look bigger. We have a biological remnant of this exact thing to this day. When you feel the hairs standing up on the back of your neck, that's your subconscious getting you ready to look as big and imposing as possible. Obviously it doesn't do much for us these days, but this is just one classic example of how we have these built in animalistic instincts that affect us to this day.

Now, as I said, you don't have to be big to be an alpha male these days. Although it does still seem to be a pretty "big" advantage. So those of us who are smaller will need to work extra hard.

If you think size only matters in the animal kingdom and that the rules of society mean that being tall doesn't count for anything, just listen to this statistic. 14.5% of the general population are over 6ft tall. Research shows that 58% of the CEO's of fortune 500 companies are over 6ft tall. I find that statistic quite amazing actually, it seems that being big can even help you get to the top in business. I would suggest however that it's not being tall that has helped them to the top. What actually helped them the fact that other people see them as more of an alpha male because of their size.

So, what can you do if you're not 6ft tall and muscular? Well you can still give off the impression that you're big without actually being big. It's all about perceptions.

Chimpanzees will stand up tall, puff out their chest and walk aggressively with their arms swaying to show that they aren't to be messed with. We can do the same, no matter what size we are. People do this all of the time without even knowing it, if you tell a child to walk like a tough guy, they will pretty much do a Chimps dominance walk without even thinking about it.

If you watch how politicians walk, they will do a similar thing. They will stand up straight, with their head up and their arms swinging at their sides to show their dominance and alpha male status.

This is a tactic you can use at any time, but it's particularly important when walking into a room to establish your presence and dominance. You will need to stride in confidently, swinging your arms, with your chest out and head high. To get the right impression.

Another tip on your stance is to not stand with your hands held together in front of you. When your hands hang like this it's called the fig leaf stance because you are effectively covering your groin with your hands. This is a typical submissive stance and is not something that an alpha male would generally do.

We have all heard about the Silverback Gorilla. When a Silverback turns about 15 years old, the hair on its back turns grey, this shows the rest of the Gorillas that he is strong and dominant.

In our culture we also see grey hair as being representative of power. Whether this is due to an instinct that is built into our brains, or due to the fact that we are taught to respect our elders from a young age and therefore associate grey hair with dominance, it's something worth keeping in mind.

Men with grey hair certainly demand more respect and are also seen as being wise. Wisdom has been an essential trait for leaders all around the world for as long as anyone can remember. So if you're going grey, just go with it!

If you really want to work on your alpha male body language and take it to the next level, a great tip is to spend more time in the company of a group of manly guys. If your current friends aren't very masculine or you hang out with a lot of women, you will be subconsciously picking up and emulating their body language when you are with them and this will have a detrimental effect.

When you are with strong, masculine men you will begin to pick up on their body language. Your subconscious will start to align itself with behaving in a similar way to these men automatically the more you socialize with them.

Another great tip is to become aware of your own body language. When you're in a social situation and you feel like you need to give off more of an alpha kind of presence, think about how you are sitting or standing and think about what that says about you.

A fast track to observing yourself is to get a friend to secretly video you as you approach a woman. It doesn't matter if you are successful or not, but watch the video back afterwards and take a look at your body language. Think about what that says about you and what impression your body language was giving off during the interaction. You may well realize some things about the way you stand or the way you walk that you hadn't noticed before.

You can then work on the aspects that you are not happy with and try again. This method will really speed up your improvement as you're essentially dropping yourself in at the deep end.

Another good tip to improve your body language instantly is to imagine you're someone else. So if you have a favorite film character who is an alpha male type, watch that film before you head into a social environment to get yourself in the zone and then act as you think they would act if they were in your shoes. Imagine you are that person and this will give you an instant body language boost.

4. FIRST IMPRESSIONS

It commonly known that first impressions count. When you're trying to give off the air of an alpha male, they count more than ever. So, we know how to walk, now let's talk about greetings.

I have heard rumors about how the handshake began. The most commonly believed theory is that the handshake originated because it was a way of showing you had no weapon on you and that your sword/gun hand was empty. I don't personally subscribe to this theory as you wouldn't actually need to touch each other to show that your hands are empty, also there is a lot of evidence for a much more convincing theory.

Apes will often, hold out their hands and touch each other's hands as a greeting. Not only this, they also sometimes even kiss the hand of the alpha male when he takes their hand. So it's highly likely that handshakes and kissing someone's hand both came from our primal instincts.

Apes will hold out their open palm to a more dominant male as a sign of reaching out in a very passive way and therefore showing their submissiveness.

Humans actually do this a lot too without even realizing it. This is because we have these subconscious actions programmed into our heads. So for example, when we are being told off by our boss or we are being challenged by another male we will often hold our palms out in a kind of confused fashion as if we are shrugging.

This is a subconscious way of reaching out for help. People will often look around to other people while showing their palms in order to show that they need assistance with the situation.

This is very common in fights between two men or when a more aggressive man is trying to pick a fight with a submissive man. The submissive man will hold out both palms and look around. This is a direct effect of our animal instincts kicking in.

When an alpha male is giving his hand to the submissive chimps who are holding their palms out to him, he will look right at them the whole time. They will bow their heads and avert their gaze. This is true of humans too, dominant and confident males will always make strong eye contact as they shake someone's hand.

Eye contact and staring is very important in establishing confidence and dominance. In many animals, a direct stare indicates a direct challenge.

Cats exhibit this behavior very noticeably. This is why cat trainers blink slowly when looking at a cat so that the cat knows the trainer isn't acting aggressively and therefore isn't a threat as he approaches.

In the ape world, a prolonged stare is seen as a challenge to the dominance of another male. So eye contact and staring has a very direct impact on how dominant we are seen by others. I actually had trouble with this one myself as I used to find it awkward making extended eye contact with people I don't know well. But I got over that and now, every hand shake is accompanied by eye contact.

It's even better if you can maintain that eye contact until they break your gaze and look away. This is a sure fire way to get them thinking you're the boss.

When an ape is confronted by a dominant male, he will put his head down in a show of submission in order to show the larger male he isn't trying to threaten the alpha's dominance. They do this in a very exaggerated an obvious way. But we still do this to an extent too. When we are in a confrontational situation and we don't want to fight, we lower our heads and look down. If you have a dog you will know that when you tell your dog off, it will lower its head as if it's cowering from you.

So when you are greeting someone, always keep your chin up and your head held nice and high and of course maintain that eye contact at all times.

Also, you should try to be the one who grabs the other persons hand and not the one offering your hand. This may seem trivial but it works. Another great tip is to twist your wrist slightly so that you are putting your hand on top of theirs, just as a dominant alpha male chimp would do. Imagine shaking someone's hand both ways and see what one would feel better to you and you will see what I mean.

There is something else that chimp's do that may also help in this respect. After two chimps finish fighting for dominance, they sometimes hug afterwards. The dominant chimp will hug the other chimp with his arms over the top of the other one and over his shoulder.

So when you hug a woman, to give of an impression of dominance, all you have to do is to hug her with your arms over hers. If you put your hands around her waist while she hugs you with her arms over the top, psychologically speaking, she will register this as submissive behavior in her subconscious mind whether she knows it or not.

So, arms over the top always for the most effective alpha male hug. This doesn't just work on the subconscious level, it works on a conscious level too. She will feel more secure and submissive when you hug her this way. If you imagine someone hugging you with your arms over your shoulders, how do you feel? Now imagine someone hugging you with their arms round your waist and you with your arms around their shoulders, how does that compare? To me, it definitely feels much more as if I am in control the second way. Having control is a huge part of being an alpha male so that's definitely a good sign.

This can be compared to putting your arm around a woman and especially putting your arm around her shoulder. It's basically a show of dominance. If you think about how it would feel for you as a man to have a woman's arm round your shoulder in public, I think most men would find that quite humiliating. Yet women actually like it. This is because it makes them feel secure and like you are a man who can watch over them, like a real alpha male.

It will also give off an air of dominance to other men when they see you with your arm around a woman's shoulders. So, be sure to try and do this more with your other half if you have one and also try doing it more on dates.

It should actually make you feel far manlier and more like an alpha male. But more importantly, it will make her think that exact same thing in a subtle way. So she won't even know what you're secretly doing.

While we're on the subject of putting your arm around a women, this works with other guys too. If you're laughing and joking with some other guys, it's pretty easy to put your arm around another guys shoulder while talking to them and joking without it looking weird. This will have the same effect on them as it would have with a woman. Also other men who see this behavior will assume you are more dominant just by seeing you do this.

We see this behavior in films all the time. When an employee is talking to an imposing boss figure he will often usher then in the direction he wants them to go by putting his hand on their back or on their shoulder and effectively pushing them about. This is a sure fire way of showing dominance.

5. BEING THE ALPHA MALE OF A GROUP

So we know how to meet people and that will get us off to a great start with establishing our alpha male status. This works great on a person to person basis and there are some tips in that last chapter that will definitely help in group situations. But if we really want to dominate a group and make ourselves the alpha male, we need to control the space in the room.

Gorillas in particular exhibit behavior relating to this exact point. When showing their dominance, gorillas will move about confidently and even barge straight through other gorillas to show that no one gets in their way.

Now I'm not telling you to run into people and shove them about, but there are more subtle ways we can use this to make people realize that we are the boss.

People exhibit this behavior very often, if you think about it, it's obvious. We have all seen it in films and most of us have probably had it happen to us before. When someone stands in your way and won't move, they are basically putting you in your place. It's a standoff and all the pressure is on you to make the next move. It's a very intimidating tactic and if you back down, you're definitely losing major alpha male points.

Luckily most people will feel uncomfortable and just move away from you whenever their personal space is invaded. We can actually use this to our advantage and to get people to move out of our way just like a gorilla would in a display of dominance.

For example, if you go up to someone in a group and you sit uncomfortably close to them on a sofa, they will most likely move up and make more room for you. This will make them feel like you are acting in a dominant way. Imagine this happening to you, someone comes and sits too close and you have to move up for them, you would feel like they were a strong presence and maybe even be intimidated by them. Using intimidation to establish dominance is the oldest trick in the book and it works brilliantly in social situations if you use it in a subtle way.

You could also do this same thing by sitting on the arm of a chair that someone is sitting in or even by leaning on a counter too close to where someone else is leaning. It all works the same way. Even walking straight between two people causing them to move for you will work.

By confidently moving around a space and causing others to move to make way for you, people will start to see you as owning the space and dominating the room subconsciously. Obviously I'm not saying to deliberately annoy people by doing this so be polite about it. Just the fact you're owning the space, even in a polite way, is enough to give off the impression that you are the alpha male in the room. It's incredibly simple really and it works.

You should see any space you're in as being your territory. Would you let someone get in your way and cause you to move in your territory? Imagine someone coming into your home and telling you to move so they could sit down.

Most of us have probably had someone tell us they were sitting somewhere, as if to tell us that we have to move before. Most of us will automatically say sorry and move straight away. But if you're thinking about any space you're in as your territory and you being the alpha male, then it's a whole different story. An alpha male can't let someone tell them where to sit, or to move and get up so they can sit down.

So protect the space you're in, if someone gets too close to you and is making you uncomfortable then tell them to take a step back. You could even make a joke that will make them look silly to the rest of the group by saying something like, "Woah. Are you trying to sit on my lap?"

Another good way to further cement your place in the group is to take the best spot, even if you don't care about it. The prime example of this is to take the front passenger seat of the car if you and some other people are getting into someone else's car.

I remember when I was a teenager, we would hang out in a group of about 20 or so people. Now I look back on it, it was very animalistic with a clear hierarchy. It was always obvious who was sitting in the front of the car whenever we went anywhere because it was whoever was considered to be the most dominant male. We didn't even need to discuss it, everyone knew who it was. So, if you can, just walk straight to the front and get in as if it's obvious you are the dominant male in the situation and other people will take note of this.

The same thing applies to seating arrangements in a room. The classic example is when the man of the house sits at the head of the dining table. I went for dinner a few times at my ex-girlfriend's parents' house. Now I think back to it, her mother was always the one who took the seat at the head of the table. It's probably no coincidence then that her husband was very submissive and just did whatever she said. The poor bloke has a pretty hard time of it and I remember feeling very sorry for him on several occasions as I watched her disrespect him.

So this behavior really does register with people. As a man and an alpha male, you should always instantly take the best, most central spot that you can straight away as if it's your right.

When you are sitting, it always helps to strike a very relaxed pose, with your arms and legs spread out in a manly fashion. This not only makes you look bigger but you will also give off an air of confidence this way.

If you combine all of this, you will dominate any space you enter and people will see you as someone that is confident and highly dominant.

Another great way to show how much of an alpha male you are in a group situation is by using your voice. This is a pretty obvious one if you think about it. Generally the more dominant males in any situation are not only more boisterous but also louder than their submissive counterparts.

By being loud and using your voice properly, you can demonstrate to others that you are confident and you are someone who will be heard. But it's not just the volume that counts.

The tone of your voice when you're exhibiting alpha male behavior is extremely important. Deep voices are associated with masculinity and are generally a good indication of body size. So, if you want to come off as being more dominant, try dropping the tone of your voice.

So make sure you own any space you are in, take the best spot and use the tone and loudness of your voice to show you are confident and dominant.

6. GIRL POWER

You might think that this is a very strange title for a chapter in a book about being an alpha male. Well, actually yeah it is pretty weird, but let me explain.

If a man has a woman with him, he is far more likely to stick up for himself in order to make himself seem stronger in front of the female.

In the animal kingdom, this is generally the whole purpose of being an alpha male. Being the alpha male means you get the ladies. Nothing is a more potent motive for males to fight for dominance than the allure of a female. The same goes for most humans too.

The problem is that nothing can kill an alpha male's stance quite as quickly as a female either. This can be done in two ways. The first way is when a male is embarrassed or shown to be weak by another male in the presence of a female. This just adds to be embarrassment of the situation. The second is when a female herself turns down or embarrasses a male. This can be either alone or even worse when it's in the company of other people.

This is probably why men are so scared of rejection from a woman. It's not just the fact that it's not nice being turned down. It's actually a direct attack on our masculinity to have a female reject us. Do you think any alpha males are getting turned down by females in the wild? Of course not. So how can we be a human alpha male if we are turned down by women? Well, it's pretty difficult.

It's also very important that you show in public that you are in control and wear the trousers if you are in a relationship. If you're out in public with your significant other and she is dominating you then you will get far less respect from anyone else who sees this happening.

We can reassert our dominance in the other ways discussed but getting turned down or being submissive towards a woman is a massive blow. So, if you're in a situation where you really need to be dominant and show you're an alpha male, you might want to steer clear of making any obvious advances towards women who might reject you, and if you have a girlfriend just make sure she knows who the boss is.

A really easy way we can get women to see us as more of a dominant male is to actually play with their children. This shows maturity and of course women will enjoy seeing you making their children smile.

Leo Turati

7. RECAP AND FINAL THOUGHTS

So to recap, here are the steps to giving off the air of an alpha male:

- Follow the alpha male code.

- Walk standing tall, with your chest out and arms swinging at your sides.

- Maintain eye contact during handshakes and try to ensure they look away before you do.

- Always hug with your arms on top and around the other person's shoulders.

- Put your arm around women's shoulders more often.

- If you're going grey, don't worry about it!

- Socialize with other dominant males to pick up on their habits and body language.

- Own the space when you're in a social environment.

- Use your voice to assert dominance and show that you are confident.

- Don't put yourself in a position where you can be rejected by a woman.

- Always make sure it's clear to others that you wear the trousers in your relationship.

Well I think that about overs it for this installment!

If you want to stay up to date with my regular free book promotions and to also find out about my future releases you can sign up to my mailing list at - www.southshorepublications.com/leoturati

If you would also consider taking the time to leave me an honest review on this book on Amazon I would be extremely appreciative of your feedback.

You can find all of my other books, full of essential advice for modern men, by simply searching for "Leo Turati" on Amazon.

Thanks for reading and I hopefully speak to you all in the next book!